WORD PLAY

TEXTURE WORDS

prickly

bristly

prickly

prickly

by Carrie B. Sheely

PEBBLE
a capstone imprint

Smooth! *Bumpy!* Fluffy!

Texture words tell you what things feel like and what they look like. Pet the sheep. Its hair is fleecy! Taste the creamy treat. Yum! Let's learn more texture words!

creamy

frothy

fleecy

syrupy

runny

sticky

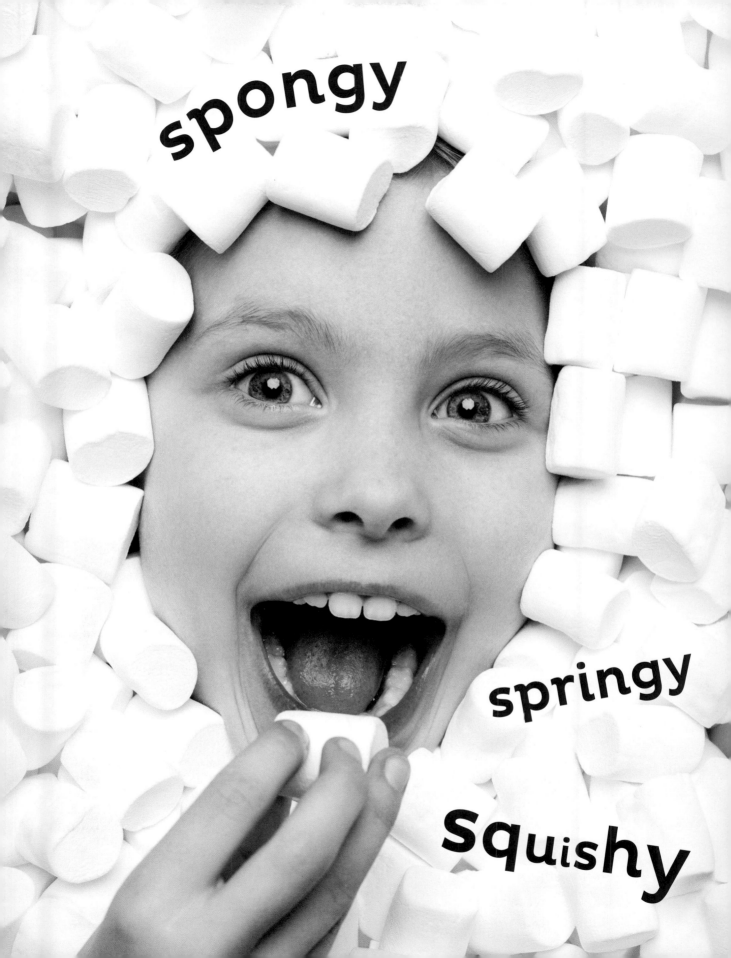

spongy

springy

squishy

foamy

coarse

gritty

grainy

frilly

scaly

dry

muddy

mucky

mushy

fuzzy

silky

puffy

spiny

spiny

spiny

sparkly

glittery

shimmery

rubbery

nubby

curly

slippery

slick

wet

stringy

chewy

gooey

greasy

leathery

smooth

pointy

thorny

spiky

powdery

stretchy

doughy

grooved

ridged

furry

crunchy

crunchy

hairy

crunchy

crunchy

hard

slimy

glossy

crispy

crumbly

fine

velvety

Pebble Sprout is published by Pebble,
an imprint of Capstone.
1710 Roe Crest Drive
North Mankato, Minnesota 56003
www.capstonepub.com

**Library of Congress Cataloging-in-Publication Data is
available on the Library of Congress website.**
ISBN: 978-1-9771-1312-2 (library binding)
ISBN: 978-1-9771-1828-8 (paperback)
ISBN: 978-1-9771-1318-4 (eBook PDF)

Summary: With engaging photos,
introduces texture words.

Image Credits
iStockphoto: martinedoucet, 3; Juliette Peters: cover, 18;
Shutterstock: Alexander Babich, 25, AnneMS, 31, Beth
Swanson, 15, bigacis, 30, bodiaphvideo, 4–5, Boryana
Manzurova, 17, Brent Hofacker, 2, Coatesy, 11, eanjoseph,
20, Elena Sherengovskaya, 10, Evgenyrychko, 16,
feelartfeelant, 19, Grigorita Ko, 26–27, Jukka Jantunen, 1,
Lawrey, 21, leolintang, 22–23, Magdalena Kucova, 6, Mark
Nazh, 7, MNStudio, 12–13, Olesya Baron, 8–9, Rawpixel, 9
(top), sashahaltam, 24, Tatiyana Koteneva, 14, Zick Svift,
28–29

Editorial Credits
Designer: Juliette Peters
Media Researcher: Svetlana Zhurkin
Production Specialist: Katy LaVigne

Printed and bound in the USA.
PA99

Titles in this set:

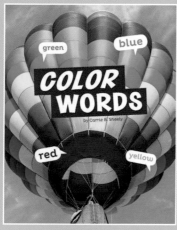

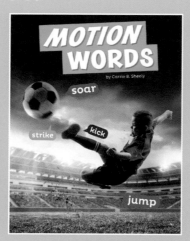

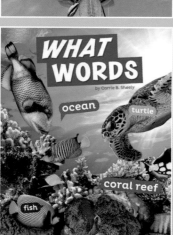

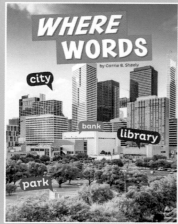